SINGAPORE
SECRET

SINGAPORE SECRET

1941 - 1981 a human story over three generations

K. S. Drake

To order additional copies of this book, contact:
Xlibris
1-800-455-039
www.Xlibris.com.au
Orders@Xlibris.com.au
795555

We know the story behind - We of the Never Never, by Jeannie Gunn; and so it was in the time of the World Wars. Twenty five million had died as a result of the first and second world war. Families were scattered; children and identity, was made up such that names were lost, missing, unknown, intopilated and somewhat drawn from history, culture and probability.

If anything was certain the most important motive was survival. Survival of the fittest.

The Australia Red Cross in its work set out to give a sense of resolution. A sense of care, compassion and value to life.

They the women, nurses, workers endeavoured to put people together reaching out to who ever could help in this time of crisis.

And one of the nurses and a worker for the Red Cross in the adoption centre after World War 2 refering to Joyce Ellen Healey, I did not know her as she died in 1955. It is only through researching family history was I able to trace this human story and information.

Kerry Susan Drake

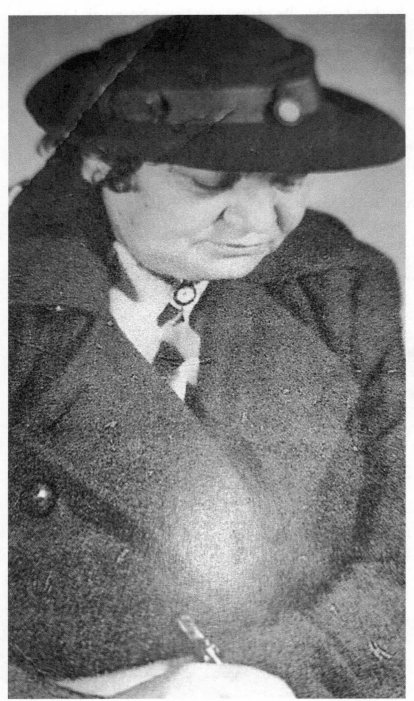

Joyce Ellen Healy
after war working
for the Red Cross

Post war and there were many widowed, war brides. As a result there were many relinquishing mothers who gave up their babies. Babies born with or without their true identity. Children were fostered by relatives under the auspices of the Red Cross. Red Cross nurses managed the adoption centre and the leading charge nurse was my Grandmother. Ellen Joyce Healey who worked tirelessly to care for the babies, parentless and unfortunately the lack of a mother. A child did die. As their situation was more desperate for they had no family to go to.

The story I am telling is of one child, named Susan who did not have a surname because the scandal of bearing a child out of wedlock. Of course Singapore war camps were so badly managed a child born in an army hospital might survive but this kind of care was never provided.

Barbara was a Singapore nurse who gave birth to a baby girl whose father served and died in Singapore after a very terrible case of bone disease. This was from being shot and the abuse of the Japanese prisoner of war camps, where thousands of soldiers from Australia suffered with British and Indian troops.

This book will be published 2020. It is a powerful moving human story about survival 1941 - 1953, the war was raging and the plight of the military forces was horrific. The Japanese never followed the Geneva Convention and rule to properly care for prisoners of war.

Why I am telling this story is because we think we are at peace now 70 years since the war ended. Yet the world is still suffering with the individual stories emerging about our war heroes in Australia.

And so the dead go on in the memory of the living.

Barbara who was a British nurse was sent to Singapore. She originally came from London. Stephen a Lance Corporal was too British and stationed in Singapore.

When it fell to the Japanese and the deaths and injured were recorded among the captured and the soldiers who were airlifted by pilots who tried to get as many home to the shores of their loved ones.

Such the like of Ron an Australian who ended up evacuating Barbara without Stephen who lie bed ridden in a rotten state.

This is the story and people who survived. The ones who did get out of Singapore. Their real names will never be known. As the battles took such great losses during the invasion of the Japanese and the fall of Singapore to the invaders.

POW: PRISONERS OF THE JAPANESE

The full story of the Australians captured by the Japanese has never been written and probably never will be. It is a horrifying story, and a tragic one. The Australian Official History tucks the fate of the POWs into 160 pages as an appendix to one of the volumes of military history. Official records state that about 7780 Australian soldiers alone died in captivity, mostly from neglect and ill-treatment at the hands of their captors, but thousands more subsequently died from their sufferings, physical and mental. Of the 22,000 Australians who fell into Japanese hands in Asia and the south-west Pacific, 35 per cent died in captivity. This was the highest percentage of any national group (25 per cent of British prisoners died in captivity) and one traceable both to the Australians' natural truculence, for which they suffered numerous reprisals, and to their physical fitness, which their captors exploited callously in forced labour.

Japanese military code – or its perversion by Bushido – regarded a warrior who surrendered as beneath contempt. (Japan had never signed the Geneva Protocol, which laid down strict rules on the proper care of

---

Australian nurses who had spent their captivity in Sumatra after liberation by Allied troops in 1945.

prisoners.) Paradoxically, Hitler's Germany generally observed the Geneva Convention in its treatment of British and American prisoners.

Japanese prisoners were treated with correctness in Allied hands. In the bloody mass breakout of Japanese prisoners at Cowra camp in 1944, 234 of them died, but the majority of the dead were suicides. During the 1943 escape attempt by Japanese at Featherston camp in New Zealand 48 prisoners were killed. Of the 18,500 Italian prisoners of war in Australia, most were employed as farm workers and few complained of ill treatment. All Italian and German prisoners of war were repatriated to their homelands by the end of 1947. 'We came as enemies,' one German officer said, 'we left as friends.'

FROM SINGAPORE TO THAILAND The 300,000 Allied servicemen and civilians captured by the Japanese (this figure includes 130,000 servicemen taken in the campaign for Malaya and Singapore and 100,000 Dutch civilians in the Indies) suffered throughout the war from shortage of food, shelter and medical treatment.

For the first few months, the British and Australian prisoners who were marched into Changi found conditions bearable. The Australian area, Selarang Barracks, was substantial, although food, beds and medical attention were inadequate, and fresh water was non-existent. (Water was brought into the camp in water carts.) POWs were given a daily ration of one pound of rice but this was later

'The Hospital': Painting of Australian prisoners on the Burma-Thailand Railway, by the artist Murray Griffin. It is part of the collection at the Australian War Memorial, Canberra.

halved, and then reduced even further. The men were 'despondent and listless', but soon had latrines dug to guard against flies and dysentery. When the men showed signs of malnutrition - avitaminosis showed as failing vision and lesions in the eyes - 120 hectares of vegetable gardens were planted, and chicken runs were established to produce eggs. Numerous activities were organised to keep the men occupied - ranging from education and language classes to entertainments, such as the Changi Concert Party. One British officer, Colonel Laurens van der Post, was astonished by the eagerness with which Australians, at Changi and in other camps, took up studies and absorbed what they learned. One prisoner remembered with a smile an Adelaide officer, Alexander Downer (a future Menzies Cabinet minister and father of a future foreign minister) giving elocution lessons to a group of working-class Diggers. The POWs originally saw few Japanese; the wire fences they were forced to erect around themselves were patrolled by renegade Sikhs.

Harsher treatment was stipulated by General Tojo in mid-1942 when he informed prison camp commandants that 'it is not necessary to be obsessed with mistaken humanitarian notions' and that prisoners must be made to work for the Emperor. May 1942 saw the first batch of working parties - Brigadier A.T. Varley's 'A' Force of 3000 men - leave camp in Singapore for an unknown destination. The Japanese assured them they were going to a place with better conditions and better food. In

farewelling them, 'Black Jack' Galleghan reminded them that 'they were soldiers, that they were men of the Anzac mould', but observers noticed that Galleghan seemed distressed, as if overcome with a sense of foreboding. Their destination proved to be the nightmare of the Burma-Thailand railway, a crazy Japanese scheme to use European prisoners and impressed native labour to build a rail through impenetrable jungle.

In July a second group, 'B' Force, consisting of 1500 men, left for Sandakan in north Borneo to construct air-fields. Other Australians, being transported by sea from places like New Britain to work in Japan or Hainan, died at sea when their ship the *Montevideo Maru* was torpedoed by an American submarine on 1 July 1942. There were no survivors among the 1000 Australian prisoners. It was the first of three transports to be sunk with prisoners aboard, to the mortification of the submariners.

In August 1942 the conditions at Changi worsened when a new commandant, Fukuye, arrived to implement a new policy of work. The prisoners unanimously rejected his demand that they sign a pledge not to attempt escape. As punishment Fukuye ordered the 17,000

Australians to stand in Selarang Barracks Square until they complied. There were only three water taps. On the same day, the Japanese forced the senior AIF officers to witness the execution – by a Sikh firing squad – of four prisoners who had attempted to escape; two of them were Australians. Three days later AIF officers ordered their men to comply with the Japanese request to sign the document, if only to avoid wholesale deaths. Escape was impossible anyway. Just to survive would take all of the men's courage and willpower. Ahead lay three years of disease, brutality and suffering in camps reaching from the steaming, monsoon-soaked jungles of Thailand to the mines of Japan.

BURMA–THAILAND RAILWAY In June 1942 the Japanese, concerned about the Allied threat to their shipping to Rangoon and the inadequacy of their roads to southern Burma, began building an overland railway. It was to run from Thanbyuzayat in Burma's south (south of Moulmein) to link up with the Thai railway system 421 kilometres away, at Bampong, near Bangkok. Work was to start from each end and meet near Nieke, using as labour prisoners of war and native people 'contracted' for the work and promised good food and pay (they received neither). They were under the supervision of Japanese engineers and guards. The 'Railway of Death' was ordered to be completed by November 1943. It was finished close to schedule, but at enormous cost in human lives and misery, and on its completion British air forces in Burma were active enough to destroy much of it in low-level bombing.

Brigadier Varley's 'A' Force began work on the railway in the north in October 1942, labouring in fierce heat with a 10-minute rest period every hour. A month later Korean guards arrived; they became notorious for their brutality. Several Australians were executed for trying to escape, and soon a third of the prisoners were too sick to work. Varley was magnificent in standing up to his captors and demanding an alleviation of his men's hardships, but deaths multiplied.

In January 1943 a second group reached Thailand. Known as 'Dunlop Force', it comprised 900 Australians captured on Java, who joined the groups pushing the railway up from the south, clearing a 3-metre-wide space for the sleepers and rails. The Bampong area was relatively flat but soon became jungle and rose into rugged hill country. To cross the River Kwai a three-tier 200-metre viaduct was built. In late 1943, 'D' Force, which included 2220 Australians, arrived from Changi to join Dunlop Force. Its commander, Lt-Colonel McEachern, wrote afterwards: 'The Japanese do not consider human life of any value when viewed in the light that the railway must be pushed on regardless of the cost ... Discipline was reinforced by brutality ...' He soon passed effective command to his junior in rank, 'Weary' Dunlop. The new arrivals were marched down river to labour on a huge embankment, working in two shifts, night and day. Next came the order to make a cutting, 500 metres long,

'WEARY' DUNLOP (1907–93)

Edward Dunlop was born in northern Victoria and was educated at Benalla High School (the school of another famous Australian, Captain Hec Waller of the Scrap Iron Flotilla). A champion footballer in his youth– nicknamed 'Weary' after the famous Dunlop tyre advertisements ('They Wear Well') – he studied medicine at Melbourne University and graduated MB BS. In 1935 he began work at Melbourne Hospital. He was working as a doctor in London when war broke out and he joined the AIF General Hospital at Palestine in 1940, serving in Greece before going on to Java with elements of the 7th Division. There he was among those who fell into Japanese hands. A towering figure, six feet four inches in height, he survived bashings and threatened execution to serve as a surgeon with his men on the Burma–Thailand Railway.

Dunlop was one of a dedicated group of doctors – Albert Coates and Kevin Fagan among them – who became a legend among the POWS. He returned to practise medicine in Melbourne after the war. In 1968 he led an Australian hospital team in Vietnam, and was knighted. His war diaries became a national bestseller. Sir Edward Dunlop died in 1993, and was accorded a state funeral.

through a hill; the cutting was later known as 'Hell Fire Pass'. Just drilling the holes in the rocks for the explosive with primitive tools left men exhausted. Others moved the rock and earth. The Australians, originally ordered to move half a cubic metre of earth a day, were soon ordered to move two cubic metres, whether they were fit or ill. The railway crept forward as the prisoners weakened, suffering from beri beri and dysentery. In late May came the wet season, the monsoon, and with it cholera in the native camps, where hygiene was primitive at best. The disease soon spread to the POWs. The indomitable doctor, 'Weary' Dunlop wrote: 'Work parades ultimately became a deplorable spectacle with men tottering with the support of sticks and carried piggy-back on to a parade ground, unable to work ...' Surgical instruments were few, anaesthetics almost unknown, and deliveries of drugs from the Red Cross by their captors rare. The death toll mounted as more POW groups were sent on from Changi. Another group, 'F' Force, including about 3500 Australians, left Bampong to march the 300 kilometres to Nieke in April 1943. By June, only 12 per cent of the 5000 men north of Nieke were fit to work, and malaria then broke out. Early in 1944, their work completed, the first Australian groups began returning to Changi. They looked like scarecrows, but they assembled in their ranks like soldiers. When 'Black Jack' Galleghan walked along the ranks of his old battalion and saw that a third of them were missing, the tears ran down his cheeks.

A total of 330,000 workers were forced to build the railway. Of the 61,000 Allied POWs who worked there, 12,399 died, including 2646 Australians and 6318 British. Up to 100,000 native labourers perished.

'They were an unruly, undisciplined, happy-go-lucky mob ... traders came padding among us hawking their boots, spoons and other superfluous items in exchange for a wad of tobacco,' recalled an English prisoner of war

The story of an unwanted pregnancy has its beginning with a relationship between a Lance Corporal, Stephen Richardson, who was stationed in Singapore at the close of the WorldWar in 1949.

A relationship that would not have happened had he not been transferred to a prisoner of war camp. Consequently the day was dawning and with the fall of the campaign to beat off the Japanese forces that surrounded the troops.

There were 8,000 Australians and Stephen Richardson who was shot and injured landing him in an army hospital. His fate was to be cared for by an English nurse who cared for him until the end of the war.

He suffered beyond a man_s limits of existence. His legacy was not known until the nurse, who had occupied his cabin and had spent nights with him, realised he could not be transported home because of malnutrition and bone decay _ had that fatal choice to stay or leave after the war and the close of the Singapore prisoner camps.

They ended their relationship with a kiss and the hope that he would recover and return to Australia.

Singapore was a death trap.

He was trapped. His nurse and lover Barbara could not stay but had to leave and there was no more work that could fund her need to be in Singapore.

When arriving back at Australian shores, it was nine months later she would have to relinquish the baby girl born in secret and transported to the Australian Red Cross as a child of the war that would be adopted out by the Red Cross by Ellen Healy Drake to a relative's family known as the Richardson family of whom Marie. Who became the bride of John Drake in June 1952. The Richardson family would be unaware that Stephen Richardson, who died eventually in 1953, had a child, a baby girl. Barbara would name her Susan. Though would not be reunited with her original mother as parent; but cared for by the cousin of the late Stephen. And became the middle child of Marie and John Drake.

A name change would occur and a new birth date using her adoption date be combined with the purpose of a new identity.

Suddenly the relative Marie Richardson had a cousin child to look after.

The idea of care for the child did have other ideations of solving the fate of the child. And it was even proposed this unwanted child was a stigma. Perhaps the best option was to dump her in the country along a forest cliff and hope a snake would eat her up. But that didn_t work as a police car saw something suspicious and thus interrupted the uncle and aunt from the shocking idea of secretly placing the baby girl who was 6 months in a death trap.

It was a difficult time 1954 and the baby Susan was never going to know her true identity.

The 50's were a cold war time and repression and children born to single mothers did not register with society and the culture of what is proper and the ideal family. The survival of women with children out of wedlock had no identity before the church and the laws of the land.

The epitaph of Stephen Richardson would be lost in time and the true mother of Susan would be a secret.

Barbara's relationship would be hidden and her life would be pursuing a relationship with a cousin of Stephen and marrying with honour and bearing three children.

The loss of her first daughter to care for and nurture would be realised when Marie Richardson turned out to be a widow. Barbara knew she had to rescue her daughter and arranged a drop in when the three children of Marie were left alone in their Carlton house. Marie became a widow and was pursued by a man from Northern Ireland working in the Snowy Mountain scheme. He pursued her and turned out to be an alcoholic wife basher.

Barbara was grieved and convinced her new relationship that if she adopted Susan this would mean she could bring the child she relinquished up in a better home.

Barbara though was faced with the fact that her husband was an alcoholic and the stresses she was under outweighed the thought even if she would do her best to care for _Susan_ in her home. It became impossible as while her three children suffered because of the devotion she had hidden for Stephen Richardson. Barbara tried to transfer that love to her husband but it was too hard. The life struggles with an alcoholic would only change when her husband was told he would die if he did not stop drinking.

The Richardson_s of her husband_s family were all prone to the disease of alcohol and sequentially died in their mid 40's.

Susan would learn of her true parents only after the longevity of her Aunt Barbara and Uncle in their mid 90's.

So life dragged on as Susan suspected her bond with Aunt Barbara was perhaps an indication of her being related.

Silence prevailed for 64 years of her life. And in the daylight after grieving the death of her Aunt Barbara was it revealed that Susan was the first child of Barbara to Stephen Richardson who died as a result of war injuries and prisoner of war camps in Singapore.

The Singapore Secret.

 The darkest memories were recorded by Susan with her identity never to be known until 2019 ' 8 months after the passing of Barbara.

As a result the search for my true identity and real father became this story. I believe I was adopted into the Drake family by Joyce Ellen Healey mother of John Raymond Hugh Drake.

A true account.

My adopted father's mother worked for the Red Cross and was the leader for placing fatherless babies into families after the Second World War.

Research

Australians atWare
A pictorial history

A K MacDOUGALL
(2007) The Five Mile Press Pty Ltd
1 Centre Road
Scoresby, Victoria 3179
Australia
www.fivemile.com.au

Original transcript
1991 as ANZACS: Australian at War.

Permission for inclusion
K S Drake Singapore Secret
2.3.2019Memoirs

more than 6000 feet, the Buffalos' fuel pump gave out, forcing the pilots to hand-pump for fuel while trying to fly the aircraft and fire their machine-guns. The remnants of 21 Squadron were evacuated after nightfall. Two days later, on 10 December, they were ordered south to Ipoh.

LOSS OF 'FORCE Z' Late in the afternoon of 8 December, as Singapore recovered from the shock of its first air raid, the newly arrived battleship *Prince of Wales* and the battle-cruiser *Repulse* left Singapore Naval Base. Moving out under grey and heavy skies, and accompanied by four destroyers, with HMAS *Vampire* in the van, they searched for the Japanese invasion armada off Singora and Kota Bharu on the far north-east coast. Admiral Phillips was informed before sailing that his ships – 'Force Z' – could not be provided in the north with air cover. On the following day he sighted three aircraft and, having found no sign of an enemy fleet, turned south. Early on 10 December, Phillips' force was attacked by waves of enemy torpedo bombers, and the two giant ships were sunk. (More than 800 British sailors died, including Phillips, but most of their men – nearly 2000 – were picked up by their destroyer escorts, which included *Vampire*.) The Dutch admiral Helfrich, commanding the Royal Netherlands East Indies Naval Forces, had placed all his units at the disposal of the British, including his large submarine flotilla, which were to score the only outstanding successes in the coming month. But in two days, Japan had destroyed the major capital ships

A Japanese painting showing the sinking of the Prince of Wales *and the* Repulse *off the coast of Malaya in December 1941.*

of Britain and America in the region. The Imperial Japanese Navy's nine battleships and 10 carriers now had absolute control of the Pacific, facing serious threat from only three American carriers, whose whereabouts was unknown.

COLLAPSE IN MALAYA

The two other Japanese landings in the north, at Singora and Patani in Thailand, had met practically no resistance. At Singora, Colonel Tsugi, the mastermind of the coming campaign, had been slightly wounded in the arm by a gendarme's bullet but Thai artillery ceased firing at noon, ending their kingdom's brief war against Japan. By nightfall of the first day, 12,000 Japanese were ashore for the loss of 500 casualties, mostly at Kota Bharu, and the loss of one ship sunk by Australian bombs.

The GOC Malaya, General Percival, anticipating a Japanese attack from Thailand, had only one brigade (of the 9th Indian Division) at Kota Bharu. The 11th Indian Division (8th and 22nd brigades) was posted in the west. The Japanese landing forces proceeded briskly to the 11th Indian Division front. They marched lightly and quickly along the roads, sometimes using bicycles, followed by light tanks. When they encountered a roadblock the infantry moved through the jungle to encircle it. Their intelligence and maps were as faultless as their flank attacks. On 12 December, the 11th Indian Division defending Jitra was outflanked and then cut in two, losing 3000 men. The division began a chaotic withdrawal to a new point 50 kilometres south. Most of these battles were fought in the rain, which turned tracks into mud.

Percival concentrated his forces in the north, but nowhere in strength. This necessitated a gradual fighting withdrawal down the length of the peninsula, absorbing brigade after brigade (and even single battalions from the Singapore Island garrison) to plug gaps in the front. These were already in flood, and would prove disastrous to Percival's troops.

The first week of fighting decided the campaign. By 10 December, the British command had lost a quarter of its aircraft and the remainder were withdrawn from northeast Malaya. The lack of fighter protection was resulting in ruinous losses in the bomber force. On the night of 12 December – by which time half of Malaya's air strength had been destroyed – the demoralised 11th Indian Division began its retreat from Jitra. By early on 14 December the depleted division was assembling at its new position, at Gurun, when it came under heavy attack and began withdrawing to a new line on the Perak River. The 9th Indian Division, withdrawn to the mid-east coast, was now to defend the Kuantan airfields. The 8th Australian Division still remained inactive in Johore, far to the south.

By 15 December, 453 Squadron – after days of tackling enemy fighters and bombers in its obsolete Buffaloes –

was down to three aircraft. After losing seven of its 12 replacements, it was ordered to join 21 Squadron (all of whose aircraft had now been destroyed) at Sembawang. Here, Group Captain John McCauley took command of its remnants, along with two RAAF Hudson squadrons and two Dutch squadrons.

By 18 December 1941, the bulk of the two Indian divisions were attempting to hold a line on the banks of the Krian River. However, a Japanese column advancing inland ('not down the roads in a straightforward fashion', as one British officer later complained) threatened their right flank, forcing a further retreat. On 19 December, the American CBS correspondent, Cecil Brown, who had survived the sinking of the *Repulse*, wrote: 'The rumours around are terrific. Everyone knows that Penang has been evacuated, but we can't say it. Refugees are streaming into Singapore. You can almost see morale collapsing like a punctured tyre ...' Penang had been hastily evacuated by the European residents, leaving the Malays and Chinese to their fate.

By 28 December 1941, the Indian and British troops had withdrawn to the Ipoh area. They repelled the enemy with great valour, but a Japanese force was now landing from small craft on the coast to their south and striking inland, threatening to cut them off. Here, the Argylls suffered heavily. Percival authorised a further retreat south to the Slim River.

Australian Bren-gunners in Malaya.

his prime, the 58-year-old Wavell found the Japanese an unpredictable enemy – one more ruthless than the Italians he had vanquished. On 17 January Wavell flew to Java to his new ABDA headquarters at Lembang, high in the hills and 105 km from Jakarta (Batavia). He was astonished to walk into a beehive of bustling Allied officers – British, Australian, Dutch and American. Only one week earlier. Admiral Hart, sent out of the Philippines in a submarine by General MacArthur, had set up naval headquarters on Surabaya at the opposite end of the island. With the death of Admiral Phillips, the departure of Admiral Layton to Colombo, and the appointment of Layton's Chief of Staff, Palliser, to Hart's command, the Australian Captain John Collins soon found himself as Commodore, Far East Squadron. He was in direct command of all British and Australian Navy units in the region. Admiral Conrad Helfrich, commanding the Royal Netherlands Navy in the Indies had already established a warm relationship with Collins, but not with the British and American admirals.

'This is the gravest hour of our history,' Prime Minister Curtin told the nation. The Japanese attack found Australia with all her trained troops – the four AIF Divisions totalling 120,000 men – overseas. She had only 15 RAAF squadrons for home defence. A total of 114,000 men were called up for the militia to bring the CMF's five infantry and two cavalry divisions to a strength of 250,000. Enlistment of militiamen in the AIF was suspended, and the first moves were made to bring the cruiser HMAS *Hobart* back from the Mediterranean to join HMAS *Perth*.

On 3 January, the British Government suggested to the Australian Cabinet that two of the Australians divisions in the Middle East be moved to the Dutch East Indies (Indonesia) from where they could be used to reinforce Malaya. On 6 January, Curtin agreed to Blamey's suggestion that the 6th and 7th Divisions be shipped to Sumatra and Java. There is no truth in the claim by British historians that 'an alarmed Australian government' demanded their return from an unwilling British War Cabinet.

'ABDA' COMMAND

To complaints that there seemed to be no co-ordinated use of Allied forces against the Japanese, a supreme Allied commander was soon appointed. One year earlier, in February 1941, President Roosevelt had convened a conference in Washington attended by American, British, Dutch, Australian and New Zealand representatives in order to lay the basis for a joint Allied command in the event of a Japanese attack. Agreement on its necessity had been achieved but little else.

'ABDA' Command (after the initials of its four major members) came into being on 6 January 1942 in an effort to co-ordinate Allied defence. General Wavell, Commander-in-Chief in India, was appointed Supreme Commander, at the insistence of the Americans who did not want one of their generals to preside over what soon promised to be a complete disaster. Stoic as ever, but past

TIME OF CRISIS: 'AUSTRALIA LOOKS TO AMERICA'

Lockheed Hudson light bombers of the RAAF over Malaya.

On 25 December 1941, the darkest Christmas in Australia's memory, Prime Minister Curtin sent to both Churchill and Roosevelt a plea to reinforce Singapore, and ordered R.G. Casey (his representative in Washington) to tell the Americans that 'the stage of gentle suggestion has now passed'. Churchill replied that he did not share the view that Singapore would fall.

On 27 December, Curtin, in an historic article in the Australian press stated: 'We refuse to accept the dictum that the Pacific struggle must be treated as a subordinate segment of the general conflict ... Without any inhibitions of any kind, I make it quite clear that Australia looks to America, free of any pangs as to our traditional links or kinship with the United Kingdom.'

This statement, the basis and guideline of Australian policy to this day, infuriated Churchill and Roosevelt, who were conferring in Washington. Churchill saw it as indicative of Australia's 'mood of panic' and was to write that it produced the worst impression both in high American circles and in Canada'. On 3 January 1942, Churchill told Curtin that he was hoping that the United States Navy would contribute to the defence of both Australia and New Zealand.

Churchill had already ordered a brigade (45th) of the 17th Indian Division and the entire British 18th Division (52nd, 53rd and 54th Brigades) to Singapore, where its main body arrived just in time to be captured. But in their conference in Washington, Churchill, Roosevelt and their Chiefs of Staff had already decided upon their strategy: 'Beat Germany first'. (Churchill would later translate this into a Mediterranean strategy of 'Beat Italy first – and then beat Germany'.) The Pacific was secondary in importance, and it was decided to fight there a defensive war. No reinforcements were sent to the Philippines, to the anguish of General Douglas MacArthur, who commanded an army of barely 20,000 American troops and 80,000 Filipino troops. MacArthur withdrew his under-equipped army into the Bataan peninsula and declared Manila an 'open city'. The Japanese entered Manila in triumph on 5 January.

There was talk of Australia and New Zealand being 'expendable', to be retrieved after the war. Nothing, in Churchill's view, must disrupt the 'Grand Alliance' he had forged with Roosevelt for their joint destruction of Nazi Germany.

On 5 January 1942, the Japanese began attacks on the Slim River position, the east-centre of the defences. Two days later, 15 of their tanks struck down the road through the 11th Indian Division (whose anti-tank guns destroyed only two of them) and penetrated to a depth of 30 kilometres behind the Indian lines. The 9th Indian Division lines in the east were also broken, and the remnants of both divisions plunged into retreat. The northern two-thirds of Malaya had now been lost.

Wavell, who had flown to the scene, approved plans for the remnants of the Indian Corps to try to hold the enemy at Kuala Lumpur before withdrawing to Johore, while the Australians moved to the west and centre. The 27th Brigade was to hold a line from Segamat to Muar (on the coast), reinforced by the 22nd Brigade – when the latter could be relieved at Mersing. On the Muar front, Bennett was also to command the 9th Indian Division (which had been strengthened by the newly arrived 45th Indian Brigade). But by 9 January, the 11th Indian Division was already endangered by enemy break-throughs and ordered to evacuate Kuala Lumpur. Within two days, the division was retreating through the

Australian lines – a disconcerting sight for the AIF men who were soon to meet to enemy.

THE 'AIF' IN ACTION: GEMAS

The Australians' first action was a spectacular one. On 14 January 1942, Lt-Colonel Galleghan's 2/30th Battalion (known by their rapid route marches in training by the nickname 'Galleghan's Greyhounds') mounted an ambush on the Gemas road that showed unorthodox tactics at their best. Hiding in the jungle on the sides of the road leading south from the bridge over the Gemenchch River, the Australians sighted several hundred Japanese troops pedalling on bicycles and let them pass. When about 1000 enemy troops had moved past them, the Australians blew the bridge, cutting off any chance of a Japanese retreat, and poured point-blank fire into them, killing hundreds before withdrawing.

The Australians halted enemy tanks by point-blank fire the next day and fell back, having inflicted an estimated 1000 casualties on the enemy for the loss of 81 officers and men. But on 16 January, the Japanese broke through Indian troops on the Muar River. The 22nd Brigade, fighting off attack at Endau on the east coast, had to send a battalion (the 2/29th) there, and to withdraw from the coastal sector. The Australian battalion found itself almost alone defending the road to Bakri, but its anti-tank gunners coolly knocked out eight Japanese light tanks with

Australian anti-tank gunners knocking out Japanese tanks with their 2-pounder near Bakri.

two-pounders. A remarkable photograph (opposite)
's these unconcerned men serving their gun while
oyed enemy tanks are burning barely 50 metres in
of them.

the night of 17 January, the situation at Muar caused
ral Bennett to sent Lt-Colonel C.G.W. Anderson's
th Battalion to reinforce the 2/29th and the embat-
45th Indian Brigade. Japanese troops striking inland
the coast quickly severed his line of retreat.
alrously waiting until Indian stragglers reached his
neter, Anderson assumed command of both AIF bat-
ns and resolved to lead the force out intact.
e fighting retreat of Anderson's force was the
mest epic of the AIF in Malaya. Forming his mixed
ralian and Indian units into a column, its trucks
ying the wounded and towing his guns, Anderson
ed off from Bakri village early on 20 January, heading
arit Sulong nearly 13 kilometres away. But they found
the Japanese had infiltrated behind them and had set
roadblock of felled trees. Anderson ordered a 'rapid
spirited assault' on it, and led the charge
self, hurling grenades. The road was cleared.
midday the column was faced by another roadblock.
ting it with point-blank fire, from the 65th Battery's
ounders, and spraying it with Bren-gun fire from
r carriers, the Australians again charged forward,
e carrying axes, and tore the block to pieces – under
nese fire all the while.
: dusk, the column rolled on to Parit Sulong. Here,
' found the Japanese had occupied the village only
rs before, when a unit of the newly arrived British
l Brigade (18th British Division) had apparently pan-
d and evacuated it. Bennett, seeing the impending
ihilation of Anderson's isolated force, demanded that
British reopen the road, but they dallied – pleading
culty in bringing up their artillery.
This day of continuing and exasperating delays by the
l Brigade ... was a day of disaster for Anderson's col-
l,' states the Australian official history. All day long on
lanuary the Australians fought off attacks from front,
· and flanks, under fire from shelling and bombing.
enceless under the avalanche of fire, the wounded lay
he ambulances and trucks standing stationary in the
t. Rejecting the Japanese order to surrender, Anderson
ered the survivors to make their own way back to
ty early on the morning of 22 January. The wounded
: to be left to the tender mercies of the Japanese. ·
l the late morning the Japanese cautiously
roached the column. They forced the 110 wounded
tralians and 40 Indians across the bridge into a shed.
night the Japanese began killing them. Trussed by
e. the captives were bayoneted or machine-gunned
l their bodies were set alight. Only a handful, feigning
th, managed to survive to tell the story.
nderson led a party to safety after a three-day struggle
ugh the jungle; it came as no surprise when this
th-African born farmer was awarded a Victoria Cross.
the 4000 men of the Muar force barely 1000 survived

The 2/19th and 2/29th battalions had lost two-thirds of
their men.

 Yet another defence line was
organised, but the Japanese
advance continued, outflanking
and overwhelming British and Indian positions before
they could be established.

As the prospect of a retreat to 'Fortress Singapore'
loomed, Percival ordered the 22nd Australian Brigade
('Eastforce') to hold Jemaluang and 'Westforce' to hold
the Kluang-Ayer-Hitani line. The 11th Indian Division,
with the 53rd British Brigade, was to hold Batu Pahat and
the coast.

In the east, the Australians at Endau and Mersing had
been attacked on 16 January, and while the 2/20th
repelled an advance on Mersing, Brigadier Taylor withdrew the rest of the 22nd Brigade to a new line south. It
was on the west coast where disaster struck. Attacked
strongly at Batu Pahat, the Indian and British troops
began to give ground and the 15th Indian Brigade was
overwhelmed. The line was stabilised only on the night
of 25 January.

On the same day, a Japanese fleet was sighted off
Lendau. In the last major attack mounted by the air force
in Malaya, nine Australian Hudsons accompanied 21 obsolete RAF Wildebeestes and three Albacores. They scored
hits on five ships, but with the staggering loss of 18 aircraft. On the following night HMAS *Vampire* and HMS
Thanet attacked the convoy, but *Thanet* was sunk.

On 24 January, the last of Westforce reached the lines of
the 2/30th at Yong Peng, the bridge was blown up, and as
Percival wrote, he 'breathed again'. Also on that day,
Australian reinforcements arrived in Singapore – the
2/4th Machine-gun Battalion (942 strong) and 2000 large-
ly untrained men whose conduct would, in many
instances, fall short of the AIF standards. Two days before
their arrival, the 44th Indian Brigade had also reached
Singapore.

The position on 25 January showed the forces in the
west still hard pressed, with the 15th, 53rd and 28th
Brigades strung out from Batu Pahat almost to Singapore
Island. Meanwhile, the 27th Brigade was counter-attack-
ing at Ayer Hitani, and Kluang was being held by the 8th
and 22nd Brigades.

Eastforce showed it still had plenty of fight left. On 26
January the 2/18th Battalion laid an ambush at the
Nithsdale Estate, 15 kilometres north of Jemaluang, its
infantry and the guns of 2/10th Field Regiment inflicting
nearly 1000 casualties on the Japanese for the cost of 98
Australian lives. But the 22nd Brigade was inevitably
ordered to fall back.

On 27 January 1942, Percival informed Wavell of the
critical situation caused by the failure of the 15th Indian
Brigade. 'The enemy has cut off and overrun the majority
of our forces on the east coast ... it looks as if we should
not be able to hold Johore for more than another three or
four days.' Wavell agreed to a withdrawal to Singapore
island, but the next day another disaster fell. The Japanese

struck the 11th Indian Division savagely. Only 200 men escaped from one of its brigades. Among the killed was Major-General Barstow, last seen making his way up a railway cutting to rally his troops. He had been one of the few British generals whom Bennett held in high regard. On 29 January, the 2/16th Battalion mounted a sudden counter-attack near Ayer Bemban after holding off attacks by three enemy battalions, and Australian gunners shelled the enemy pushing forward. The Japanese battle report stated that 'the enemy, defying death, strangely and impudently counter-attacked with bayonets along the entire line'. The Australians still had a lot of fight left in them.

General Wavell flew into Singapore on 30 January 1942, and there conferred with his commanders, ordering all air force squadrons (except one) to fly to Sumatra. Afterwards, Major-General Bennett drove through the deserted streets of Johore Bharu and past their bombed buildings. He wrote: 'This defeat should never have been. The whole thing is fantastic. There seems to be no justification for it.' He had already determined that if Singapore fell he would make his way to Australia and impart what he had learned from the bitter lessons of the campaign to the Australian government.

Now began the retreat to Singapore island, the last bastion. On 31 January 1942 the last British unit - the remnants of the Argyll and Sutherland Highlanders, barely 90 strong - marched across the causeway to the skirl of the pipes. Shortly afterwards, the link to the mainland was blown, leaving a 70-metre gap. Destroyed with it was the pipeline bringing fresh water to Singapore. The Strait was to prove an ineffective moat. At low tide parts of it were only 1.3 metres deep.

Newspapers told of a fighting retreat caused by 'overwhelming numbers of Japanese', but the enemy had conquered Malaya with only 35,000 men. This number had been enough to drive an army of 60,000 defenders into a humiliating 1000-kilometre retreat. Japanese casualties were barely 1793 killed and 2772 wounded.

The conquest of Malaya was the greatest victory for the Japanese in nearly two months of astonishing success. On 26 December, Hong Kong had surrendered. On 11 January, the Japanese had invaded Borneo, and on 15 January, Burma. On 25 January the Japanese had attacked Rabaul, and Ambon five days later. There seemed no end to this cyclone of calamity.

The American authority on Japan at war, David Bergamini, writes:

'The Australians had fought well. They had taken the offensive, infiltrated, ambushed, and dispelled the growing notion that the Japanese were peculiarly, demonically, at home in the jungle. In the last 10 days the Australians had inflicted heavier losses on Yamashita's men than they had suffered earlier or would suffer later.

'With another division as good as the Australians, Percival might have held the line, for by now the Japanese attackers were themselves hungry, footsore and sick. But gaps in the Australian position were plugged with Indian troops who had already been chased south

for 400 miles. The plugs broke and Percival had no choice but to fall back on Singapore.

'The Australian troops, for the most part, were disappointed, because they were still fresh and had so far outfought the Japanese ...'

What was going wrong with S~

Singapore was a fortress in name only, its northern shores lacking fixed defences, a naval base without a fleet. Informed of Singapore's lack of defences, Churchill was to write in his memoirs: 'No measures worth speaking of had been taken by any of the commanders since the war began...I saw before me the spectre of the almost naked island and of the wearied, if not exhausted, troops retreating upon it.' In mid-January 1942 he had cabled Wavell: 'I want to make it absolutely clear that I expect every inch of ground to be defended ... and no question of surrender entertained until after protracted fighting among the ruins of Singapore City.'

On 21 January, however, he informed his Chiefs of Staff: 'We may, by muddling things through and hesitating to take an ugly decision, lose both Singapore and the Burma Road. If Singapore lasts only a few weeks it is not worth losing all our reinforcements and aircraft.'

Sensing what the 'ugly decision' might be, Prime Minister Curtin cabled Churchill on 23 January, demanding that Singapore be held with all available resources. It is an accurate reflection of Australia's fears and disillusionment: 'After all the assurances we have been given, the evacuation of Singapore would be regarded here as an inexcusable betrayal. Singapore is a central fortress in the system of Empire and local defence ... We understand that it was to be made impregnable ... or be capable of holding out for a prolonged period until the arrival of the main fleet.'

Singapore's peace-time population of 700,000 people had now swollen to nearly a million by countless thousands of refugees and more than 100,000 troops. The island, barely 40 kilometres long and 20 kilometres wide, had drawn its main water supplies from Johore, but now that the pipeline had been cut, the reservoirs were barely adequate to support the extra mouths. There were air raid shelters for some Europeans, but none for Asians. On some days, Japanese bombing in February would claim nearly 2000 casualties. Food stocks were dwindling, but stores, hotels and cinemas remained open, providing an illusion of normality. The Chinese community provided willing helpers to the ARP services and to teams digging slit trenches, and numerous volunteers for Lt-Colonel John Dalley's force of irregulars - ill-armed but willing to fight to the death against the Japanese.

'The battle of Malaya has come to an end,' General Percival announced, echoing Mr Churchill, on 1 February 1942, 'and the battle of Singapore has started ... Our task is to hold the fortress until help can come.' Convoys continued to make the 500-mile voyage from Sunda Strait to Singapore, mostly under cover of night. Captain Collins, having received first-hand reports of the chaos on the docks where war material was lying looted or uncrated, protested to Wavell that it was absurd to waste lives in sending further convoys to the city. Wavell ordered the next convoy to go through. On 5 February a five-ship convoy carrying 2000 AIF reinforcements (most of them on the liner *Empress of Asia*) came under terrific enemy air attack and the liner was one of two ships left burning and sinking. However HMAS *Yarra* rescued 1800 of the men she was carrying. It was the last convoy to reach Singapore.

SINGAPORE: PREPARING FOR INVASION

Invasion was expected daily, but where would the Japanese land? The unfortified northern coast seemed the logical choice, but the enemy's ability to land seaborne forces caused Percival to distribute his forces around the island's 120-kilometre perimeter. In the words of the British official historian: 'In trying to defend the whole coast when it was obvious the Japanese would concentrate on one carefully selected point, Percival was weak everywhere, no formation had any reserves for immediate counter-attack ...'

Percival divided the northern coast into two sectors and selected the 8th Australian Division to defend the 'West' as far as the Causeway. 'I had specially selected it for the Australian Imperial Force ... because ... it was the freshest and the more likely to give a good account of itself.' Its two brigades were separated by the Kingi River.

The Island's 'East' was the responsibility of 3 Indian Corps (the 11th Indian Division) plus the 18th British Division, now complete with the arrival of its last two brigades on 29 January.

Singapore was now under constant artillery bombardment, but the great guns of the fortress could make little response: lack of high explosive shells, and problems of 'location, lack of range, or limited traverse' negated their use.

Percival allotted the bulk of his artillery to the eastern sector. In the Australian sector only five per cent of the frontage could have artillery support at any given time. Bennett received reinforcements at last: the 2/19th alone absorbed 500 new members, but the majority of them were untrained.

THE FALL OF SINGAPORE

On 8 February 1942, Japanese shelling increased in intensity on the northern coast as 16 battalions of infantry prepared to cross the straits. Communication lines were broken by shelling. The bombardment woke Bennett who, on reaching his headquarters at 1.30 a.m. heard from Brigadier Taylor that 'penetration had occurred' on his 22nd Brigade front.

The assault, in the first hour of 9 February, had fallen on the 2/20th, 2/19th and 2/18th, and the Australians poured fire into the Japanese, clambering from barges and groups assembling on the beaches. The defenders fought stubbornly, hurling grenades and often fighting hand to hand, but their positions were overcome or bypassed. Bennett called up the widely dispersed 2/29th, his reserve, but by

Japanese photo of General Percival (far right) and his officers, carrying the Union Jack and the white flag, arriving to negotiate the surrender of Singapore, 15 February 1942.

無條件投降,背簽字的顧史的揖基··· 簽字的是巴息●蒙軍司令官·對面左端是日本山下奉添指揮官。

dawn the position of the 22nd Brigade was desperate and units were falling back to Tengah airfield, the Japanese objective. An attack on the airfield was repulsed by the 2/18th's carrier platoon. Percival ordered up the 12th Indian Brigade to support Bennett, who ordered his forces, plus the 44th Indian Brigade in the south-west to fall back if in danger of being cut off, to the new defence line running from Kranji in the north to Jurong. The 6/15th Indian Brigade was to defend Bukit Timah. On returning to his headquarters, Percival told Bennett and Lt-General Heath of the Indian Corps that if the Japanese reached the Bukit Timah road he would fall back and make a tight perimeter around Singapore city.

Meanwhile, Brigadier Maxwell of 27th Brigade, assuming that the 22nd Brigade had been overcome and that his left flank was exposed, obtained permission to withdraw from the Causeway position to a stronger line, three kilometres south. However, at 9 p.m., on 9 February, the Japanese Imperial Guards were crossing the straits to fall upon the 27th Brigade. The 2/30th brought down mortar fire on the enemy seen clambering out of boats at the mouth of a creek. By midnight the 2/26th was fighting near Kranji village. At 4.30 a.m. the sound of fighting was

General Percival signs the unconditional surrender of Singapore. Seated opposite him is General Yamashita, who refused to discuss any concessions.

drowned by the explosion of two million gallons of fuel as the Naval Base was destroyed by Australian sappers. The flaming petrol poured down the Straits, consuming barge-loads of Japanese. When horrifying stories of this reached the Guards commander, General Nishimura - suddenly squeamish - called off further attacks across the water. Over Singapore hung a dark and thickening black cloud.

By the morning of 10 February, Bennett felt confident that the dispositions along the Kranji-Jurong line were enough to hold the enemy. But then a succession of misinterpretations of Percival's decision to withdraw to Singapore city occurred - causing the entire line to be abandoned by nightfall.

Seeing the 22nd Brigade withdrawing, the 12th Brigade similarly fell back, to a position on the Bukit Panjang crossroads. The 6/15th and the 44th Brigades also retreated. In the north the 11th Indian Division was equally perplexed by the withdrawal of Maxwell's 27th Brigade.

Wavell again flew into Singapore, arriving on 10 February. He criticised Percival for allowing the Japanese to establish themselves and ordered him to counter-attack and retake the Kranji-Jurong line early in the afternoon. Wavell became so exasperated with Bennett's remarks that he told him to 'get the hell out' and take his 'bloody Aussies' with him. Wavell issued an order to his troops stating:' We must defeat them ... The Americans have held out on the Bataan Peninsula against far greater odds ... It will be disgraceful ... if we yield our boasted fortress of Singapore to inferior enemy forces.' In London, General Sir Alan Brooke, who had taken over as CIGS only a week before Pearl Harbour was attacked, noted in his diary next day:'The news of Singapore goes from bad to worse ... I certainly never expected we would fall to pieces as fast as we are.'

Thus, by the evening of 10 February, the battle-weary defenders were holding the line running the length of Woodlands road against Japanese thrusts from both north and east. The counter-attack failed and enemy tanks now appeared. The Japanese had reached the outskirts of Bukit Timah village by 10.30 pm. On the morning of 11 February, Bennett ordered the enemy driven from its environs; a motley force was scratched together to defend the reservoirs. On this day, the first group of Australian nurses was evacuated from Singapore on the *Empire Star*, which made it through to Java. The second group was not so fortunate.

Disasters multiplied. Brigadier Maxwell informed Major-General Key of the 11th Division that he had been ordered by Percival to withdraw further south and recapture Bukit Panjang village, where hard fighting had taken place the previous day. Whoever issued the order – Percival denied doing so – was responsible for a disaster. Seeing the 11th Division's left flank completely exposed, General Heath ordered 3 Indian Corps to withdraw from the north coast, abandoning the naval base, to establish a new continuous line further south.

On 12 February, General Yamashita dropped courteously worded demands for Singapore's surrender. Percival sadly ordered a withdrawal to a 'tight perimeter' around Singapore city, urging Heath to defend the reservoirs north of the city with the 11th and 18th Divisions. That day Brigadier Taylor collapsed after days without sleep and was replaced by Lt-Colonel Varley. The remnants of the two Australian brigades were still holding 12 kilometres of front.'I consider that the end is very near,' Bennett wrote in his diary. The Japanese were now only five kilometres from the docks and were shelling the city with field artillery. On 13 February, Percival met his commanders at Fort Canning. From Bennett and Heath, Percival heard that there was no chance of mounting a counter-attack. Rear-Admiral Spooner ordered all naval vessels to leave Singapore to avoid capture, and Air Vice-Marshal Pulford was ordered to accompany him to Java. 'I suppose you and I will be held responsible for all this,' Pulford said to Percival, 'but God knows we did our best with what little we had been given.' (Both Spooner and Pulford were to die lingering deaths after their vessel

was driven ashore days later on one of the Thousand Islands.)

Friday 13 February 1942 would be remembered in Singapore as 'Black Friday'. Eighty small craft sailed out of the harbour, leaving behind a city burning under a pall of black smoke. Few of them made it past Japanese surface patrols.

On 14 February, Japanese tanks and infantry reached the pumping station and the reservoirs. Others entered the Alexandra Barracks Hospital, where they the next day bayoneted 100 of their prisoners, nearly all of whom were patients or medical staff. Told that the water supply would last only 48 hours at best, Percival, on 15 February, informed Wavell of his intention to seek a ceasefire.

At 5.15 p.m. on 15 February 1942, General Percival, accompanied by a small group of officers carrying a white flag and the Union Jack, met General Yamashita at the Ford factory on the outskirts of Singapore city, and was informed that his total and unconditional surrender was demanded. The capitulation was signed forthwith, the surrender to be effective from 8.30 p.m. the same day.

In what Prime Minister Churchill was to call 'the greatest disaster to British arms which our history affords,' the battle of Malaya and Singapore ended. A total of 130,000 men passed into Japanese captivity. Of this number 67,340 were Indian; 38,496 British; 18,490 Australian; and 14,382 were local volunteers. In the entire campaign the British command had suffered 8000 casualties (killed and wounded). Japan's losses were 9824 of whom 3500 were killed. Australian losses included 1789 killed and 1306 wounded. Before victory over Japan, nearly 8000 Australian prisoners would die in the hands of their captors.

Some escaped. Major-General Bennett handed over command of the 8th Division to his artillery commander, Brigadier Callaghan, and with two of his staff officers – Moses and Walker – got away from Singapore just after midnight. They crossed to Sumatra and then Java and thence by plane to Australia. Bennett stated his motives thus:'I must at all costs return to Australia to tell our people the story of our conflict with the Japanese, to warn them of the danger to Australia and to advise them of the best means of defeating Japanese tactics.' Bennett met a glacial reception from his government and never again held a field command. But when the remnants of the 8th Division returned from captivity in 1945, Bennett, dressed in civilian clothes, was there at the dock to meet them. The depth of their regard for him and their belief in the sincerity of his motives eased the hurt of his later years.

Others sought to escape but failed. Mr. V. Bowden, the Australian government's representative in Singapore, was captured by the Japanese, ill-treated (despite his diplomatic status), forced to dig his own grave and executed two days after the fall of Singapore. On 14 February, the 65 Australian nurses evacuated from the city two days earlier on the *Vyner Brooke* met with tragedy when the ship was bombed and sunk. A group of 22 survivors was captured by a Japanese patrol on Banka Island, forced to walk into the surf, and machine-gunned. Only one nursing sister, Vivian Bullwinkel, survived.

'The surrendered army was a mournful sight,' one young Chinese student in Singapore, Lee Kuan Yew, later wrote, after watching the defeated troops trudge into captivity. 'The Australians looked dispirited, not marching in step. The Indian troops, too, looked dejected and demoralised. They must have felt this was not their fight.' Singapore's future Prime Minister never forgot the sight of the Scots, whom he recognised by their Highland caps and bonnets: 'Even in defeat they held themselves erect and marched in time'. The Gurkhas also marched with shoulders back, 'erect, unbroken and doughty in defeat. I secretly cheered them.'

Japanese fury fell on the Chinese, rather than the Malays, few of whom welcomed the new regime. The Chinese communities were spread throughout south-east Asia, and their hatred for the Japanese was deep. Through the grim years ahead the Chinese were the first to help Allied prisoners with food and form the core of resistance groups. In the early weeks of the Japanese occupation of Singapore, thousands of members of the Chinese community were massacred by the Japanese. It began on 18 February when all Chinese males between 18 and 50 were ordered to present themselves at a series of collection points. The Japanese, among them members of the dreaded secret police, the Kempei, then picked out several thousand at random and transferred them to the grounds of Victoria School. On 22 February, 50 lorries began picking them up and taking them to a beach near Changi prison, where they were machine-gunned and the survivors bayoneted to death. A senior officer flew out from Tokyo to investigate rumours of the killings and described them not as 'reprisals' but 'atrocities'. After the war, the Japanese admitted to the killing of 6000 Chinese. However, after exhuming the bodies, a committee found evidence of a massacre of more than 50,000 civilians. Of the 67,000 Indian troops captured, well over 40,000 were coerced into renouncing their allegiance to the Crown and joining the Japan-sponsored 'Indian National Army' (INA). Few of them joined willingly and the INA, woefully under-equipped, later fought without enthusiasm against the British-Indian army in Burma.

'I saw a social system crumble suddenly before an occupying army that was absolutely merciless,' Lee wrote in his memoirs. 'Once the Japanese lorded it over us as conquerors they soon demonstrated to their fellow Asiatics that they were more cruel, more unjust and more vicious than the British. During the three and a half years of the occupation, whenever I encountered some Japanese tormenting, beating or ill-treating one of our people, I wished the British were still in charge.' The Japanese 'Co-Prosperity Sphere' would witness the death of millions of native people from starvation or brutality – nearly 50,000 Malays, more than 100,000 Filipinos and nearly two million Indonesians (the last mostly died in a cruel forced labour scheme).

THE BURMA CONTROVERSY

The defences of Burma were now collapsing before the Japanese advance. On 20 February the division defending Rangoon on the east bank of the Sittang River was marooned by the premature demolition of the bridge to the west bank. Churchill was aware that now nothing stood between the Japanese and their goal – Rangoon. So, on 21 February 1942, without informing the Australian Prime Minister, he ordered the leading convoy carrying a brigade of the returning 7th Australian Division, then rounding Ceylon, to make for Rangoon. In Churchill's mind the only troops close enough, and capable, of holding Rangoon and southern Burma were the Australians.

Curtin was astonished by Churchill's action and – in an angry cable on 23 February – protested to him: 'Australia's outer defences are now quickly vanishing and our vulnerability is completely exposed . . .With AIF troops we sought to save Malaya and Singapore, falling back on the Netherlands East Indies. All these northern defences are gone or going, now you contemplate using the AIF to save Burma. All this has been done, as in Greece, without adequate air support.' The convoy was immediately ordered back on its original course, towards Colombo. Curtin later agreed to two brigades of the returning 6th Division remaining in Ceylon for a period (They arrived late in March and were kept in Ceylon for four months, when they were desperately needed in New Guinea.) This, and his decision not to press for the recall of 9th Division from the Middle East, was the extent of his compromise.

'But if we could not send an army,' Churchill was to write, 'we could at any rate send a man.' Churchill asked Britain's youngest Lieutenant-General, Alexander, who had commanded the rearguard at Dunkirk, to fly to Rangoon and sort out order from chaos. Alexander left England on the night of 28 February for the perilous flight to Burma, accompanied only by his aide-de-camp, a 22-year-old Australian holding a commission in the Irish Guards, Captain Rupert Clarke. They arrived in Rangoon on 5 March to find the city under a pall of smoke from demolitions and air raids, the Japanese close to cutting it off from the north. After the failure of a counter-attack on 6 March, Alexander ordered his troops to evacuate Rangoon the next day, and fought his way through enemy roadblocks just as the first Japanese troops entered Rangoon (8 March). 'Alex', with Lt-General William Slim as his Corps commander (hastily flown to the scene from Iraq), was to lead the army on what would be a nightmare two-month, 1600-kilometre fighting retreat to Imphal on the mountain border of India. A race against the May monsoon, his progress was slowed by 150,000 Indian refugees, one-third of whom were to perish on the way. Churchill persisted in believing that the arrival of the Australians could have saved Burma. Nothing could have saved Burma in February and March 1942.

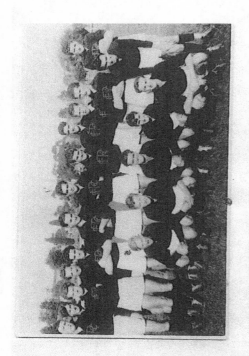

John R. H. Drake

The Drake's in Australia
As told by John's daughter Kerry

Our first settlers came out on the Ship Flora in October 1852 sailing from Liverpool; stopping at Port Henry and eventually settling in Allansford establishing a dairy industry.

Hugh Drake married Ann Jane Martin and sailed on the ship Flora, 21-7-1852 arriving at Port Henry 23-10-1852.

Hugh was born in County Down Ireland.

They brought with them their six children William 16 yrs, Margaret 14 yrs, John 12 yrs, James 10 yrs, Hugh 5 yrs and Thomas 3 yrs.

Hugh was an Agricultural laborer and a native of County Down's Ireland and a follower of the Church of England.

William his oldest son born in Townsland Glough, (our great grandfather) married Elizabeth Perkins 8 August 1860, at Englwood Cottage, Inverliegh. Their children were Mary Ann, Jane and Hugh, (our great grandfather) born 12 December 1865, in Allansford, Victoria, Australia. Emily was born on the 4 October 1867 Wagoon, Victoria and her parents were William Bolden and Elisabeth Harris. Hugh and Harriet had four children, Ethel, Herbert, Ephraim and Arthur. Arthur our grandfather was born 9 Febuary 1900 and married Joyce Ellen Healey 3 July 1918. Arthur Joseph Drake of Warragul, Victoria was the father of seven children: George Alfred, Rosa Mabel, Melva Francis, John Raymond Hugh, Terrence James, Ronald Maxwell and Joyce Alwin.

John R. H. Drake is the father of Cheryl, Kerry and Michelle through marriage to Marie E. Richardson 14 June 1952 at St. Joseph's Collingwood. John was born 13 October 1928 in North Melbourne and died aged 33 years, after sustained injuries received in a car accident that occurred 12 months earlier.

He died of brain damage at Mont Park Hospital.

∞

John's Grandfather ~ Hugh Drake

John's Mother ~ Joyce Ellen Healey
John's eldest brother ~ George Alfred Drake

John's Mother ~ Joyce Ellen Healey

A Mascot for the Collingwood Football team

Please
give
this little
bird some
wings.

*John begins his career in football whilst
at Collingwood Technical school*

*Educated at Collingwood Technical school
John left school at the age of 16.*

Nº 429337

Education Department,

VICTORIA.

MERIT CERTIFICATE

This is to Certify

that _John R H Drake_

has completed satisfactorily the Course of Study

prescribed for _Junior Technical Schools_

Dated at _Collingwood_ School

this _12th_ day of _November_ A.D. 1943

_____
Head Teacher.

_____
Inspector of Schools.

FIRST YEAR 19				SECOND YEAR 19				THIRD YEAR 19			
SUBJECTS	HALF YEAR RESULTS			SUBJECTS	HALF YEAR RESULTS			SUBJECTS	HALF YEAR RESULTS		
	1	2	TOTAL		1	2	TOTAL		1	2	TOTAL
English	7	77	163	English		73	127	English		61	128
Social Studies		74	147	Social Studies	63	67	130			72	113
Arithmetic		54	120	Arith. Book-keep	63	60	123			72	99
Algebra				Algebra	77	62	139	Science	57	45	103
Science		26	67	Science	48	48	96	Science II		60	121
Mech. Draw		59	115	Free Hand		70	133	Solid Geometry		72	118
Modelling		82	136	Modelling				Mech. Drawing		74	156
		85	128	Solid Geometry	42	84		Wood Theory			
Woodwork		72	141	Mech. Drawing	56	81	115	Woodwork			
Elect	70	76	136	Mech. Shop Pract		76	162	Mech. Shop Pract	57	65	122
				Woodwork		70	134	Fitting Theory			
				Elect. Fitting	86	69	155	Elect. Fitting	56	61	127
				Sheetmetal							
TOTAL	63	605	1143	TOTALS	834	827		TOTALS		746	1072
Average	60	672		Average	70	67		Average		64	
Order of Merit				Order of Merit		15		Order of Merit			
Students in Form				Students in Form		26		Students in Form		26	
Form II				Form II				Form II			

FORM	SUBJECT		MARKS OBTAINED									
			MID TERM	FINAL TERM		1st TERM		2nd TERM		3rd TERM		
	Maths					8	2					
						10	12					

PREMIERS   PREMIERS

COLLINGWOOD FOOTBALL CLUB

FLOREAT   PICA

SCHOOLS COMPETITION

Premiership Certificate

Master   *John Drake*

was a member of The Collingwood Technical

School Football Team, winners ———

"B" Grade Premiership —— Season 1942.

On behalf of the Collingwood Football Club,

_____ President.

_____ Hon. Treasurer.   _____ Hon. Secretary.

_____ Schools District Secretary.

Married at St Joseph's

Ted + Jean   John + Myra   Henry   Rosa   George
Bourke   Drake   Richardson Richardson Drake   Drake

In the State of Victoria. In the Commonwealth of Australia.

FOURTH SCHEDULE, ACT No. 3725 and ACT No. 3764.— FORM B.

CERTIFICATE OF MARRIAGE

[B

Year 19__. Parish or Church District _____ Collingwood _____ Denomination _____ Catholic _____

No. in Register. **(1.)**		133
When and where Married. **(2.)**	June 14th 1952	
	St Joseph's Collingwood	
Name and Surname of each Party. **(3.)**	John Raymond Single Casby	Anna Ciani Constantino
Conjugal Condition, also date of Decease of each former Spouse (if Widowed), or date of Order Absolute (if Divorced). **(4.)**	Bachelor	Spinster
Children by each former Marriage. Living. **(5.)**		
Dead. **(6.)**		
Birthplace. **(7.)**	East Melbourne	Italy
Occupation. **(8.)**	Labourer	Dress Machinist
Age in years (last Birthday). **(9.)**	23 years	24 years
Exact Residence of each Party. Present. **(10.)**		
Usual. **(11.)**		
Parents' Names. Father. (Also occupation.) **(12.)**		
Mother. (Full Maiden Name.) **(13.)**		

We declare that the above is a true statement of the particulars relating to each of us respectively; and that Marriage _____ was solemnized between us on the date and at the place mentioned, according to _____

ℬ𝓞 John Raymond Hugh Drake age 23 ℂ𝓡
℘ Married ℘
ℬ𝓞 Marie Elsa Richardson age 19 ℂ𝓡

Ellen Joyce   John   +   Myra   Arthur Joseph
Drake   Drake
nee Healey

Dad & Mychelle

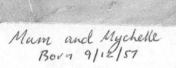

Mum and Mychelle
Born 9/12/57

Kerry Susan & Cheryl
Born 24/11/54   Born 15/8/53

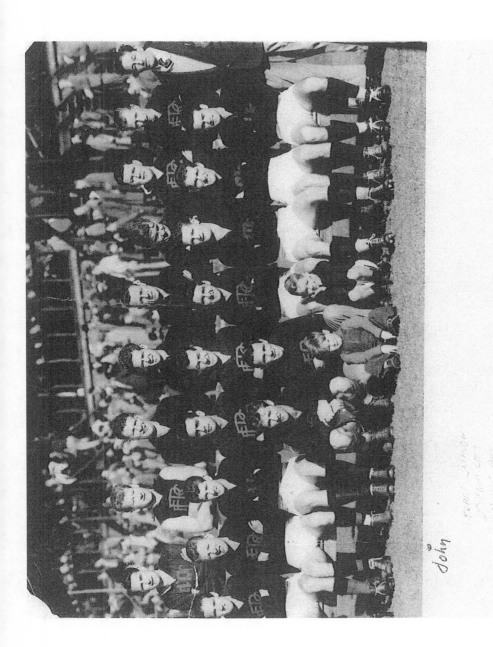

John

PERCY JACKSON
BACK AS LEFT
2ND FULL BACK
2ND FULL BACK
1 RIGHT WING

VICTORIAN TRAMWAYS FOOTBALL ASSOCIATION

The interstate Carnival was held in Adelaide. New South Wales did not make the trip owing to the inability to field a side. The Victorians arrived in Adelaide on Sunday, July 29th. They were met on arrival by officials of Adelaide Tramways Football Club. After lunch visitors were taken for a bus ride round the city and suburbs. Monday, a reception by the M.T.T. and in the evening were guests of A.E.T.C. Social at Hackney Hall. Tuesday, a full day trip to Victor Harbour. Wednesday, National Football Council meeting at which two Life-Governors were elected J. Ferguson (Vic.) and J. Spence (Adelaide). The match was played on the Wednesday afternoon, Victoria being the winners.
Final scores: Victoria 11.14 to South Aust. 11.6.

The best player of the Carnival was M. Drake (Vic.) with A. Tume (S.A.) runner-up.
Thursday, guests of the Old Comrades Association on a full day tour of the hills. Friday, guests of Tramways Football Club at a Social in the Hackney Hall. The Sir William Goodman Shield and the Bunny Curtain Cup were handed over to the the Manager of the Victorian side Reg Hodder. Saturday guests of the South Australia National Football League and Gawler Jockey Club. Sunday, guests of North Adelaide Football Club and we were pleased to meet Haydn Bunton who was present. At 7 p.m. visitors departed for home after one of the most enjoyable Carnivals ever.
The news of the death of Herb Grant of Sydney came as a great shock to this Association. Herb was a Past President and Manager of many New South Wales football teams. He

Newspaper clippings about John

Three nominations for Coach. Last year's coach, B. Carpenter, Mick Drake from Essendon and Brian Wells from Brunswick. Brian Wells was appointed. Congratulations Brian, the committee and the players are behind you. The players are looking forward to the first match with Mickey Drake, who won the Best and Fairest twice in the Tramways Competition, and Brian Wells, who was vice-captain of the Victorian side last year, and with a lot of young recruits. This side could win a lot of games this year, and not forgetting that fine combination (Max, Joe and Tom).

Players, do not forget these practice days. Watch the Notice Board for same and make it your business to be there.

Victorian Tramways

The final boto consisted of Essendon, Malvern, Glenhuntly, Port and Central Bus. Port won the easy semi final. Malvern-Glenhuntly the second, the surprise being the defeat of Essendon, the best for the year.

Essendon ran out an easy winner in the Preliminary Final. The scores being Essendon 8-5, Port 3 points. Malvern and Essendon now play the Grand Final.

The best and fairest for the Association was M. Drake (Essendon), runner-up B. Wells (Brunswick). The Interstate Carnival was a great success. The Visitors arrived by the "Overland" on Sunday 14th August and were met by the President and Secretary and members of the Executive.

Monday 15th August they were the guests of the Tramways Board at Luncheon in the Wattle Park

John Also enjoyed cricket as a young sports man

John's nickname became "Micky," because of his great love for Mickey mouse.

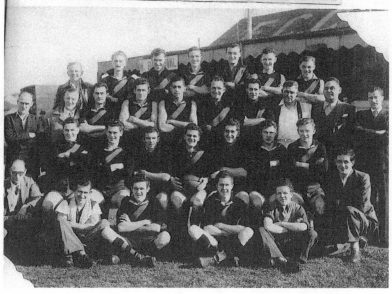

Family Group Record

HUSBAND JOHN RAYMOND HUGH DRAKE

Born	13 OCT 1928	Place
Chr.		Place
Marr.	14 JUN 1962	Place COLLINGWOOD, VICT. AUST
Died	26 MAR 1962	Place
Bur.	28 MAR 1962	Place SPRINGVALE CEMETERY

HUSBAND'S FATHER ARTHUR JOSEPH DRAKE

HUSBAND'S MOTHER JOYCE ELLEN HEALEY

HUSBAND'S OTHER WIVES

WIFE MYRA ELSA RICHARDSON

Born	24 APRIL 1933	Place DIGGERS, VICT.
Chr.		Place
Died		Place
Bur.		Place

WIFE'S FATHER HENRY RICHARDSON

WIFE'S MOTHER ELSIE CLAUDINE MUSTARD

WIFE'S OTHER HUSBANDS

SEX M/F	CHILDREN List each child (whether living or dead) in order of birth Given Names SURNAME	WHEN BORN DAY	MONTH	YEAR	WHERE BORN TOWN	COUNTY	STATE OR COUNTRY	DATE OF FIRST MARRIAGE TO WHOM	WHEN DIED DAY	MONTH	YEAR
1	CHERYL MARIE	15	AUG	53	CARLTON, MELB	VIC	AUST				
2	KERRY SUSAN	24	NOV	54	"	VIC	"	6 NOV 8?- Robert Richard Mason			
3	MICHELLE CAROL	9	DEC	57	"	VIC	"	Robert Pens			
4											
5											
6											
7											
8											
9											
10											
11											

OTHER MARRIAGES

SOURCES OF INFORMATION

Husband

Wife

Ward

Examiners 1

2

Stake or Mission

HUSBAND ARTHUR JOSEPH DRAKE

Born	9 FEB 1900	Place WARRAGUL, VICT. AUST
Chr		Place
Marr	3 JULY 1919	Place
Died	21 JULY 1969	Place
Bur.		Place

HUSBAND'S FATHER HUGH DRAKE
HUSBANDS OTHER WIVES
HUSBAND'S MOTHER HARRIET EMILY BOLDEN

WIFE JOYCE ELLEN HEALEY

Born	29 MAR 1900	Place
Chr		Place
Died	3 JAN 1955	Place MELB. VICTORIA. AUST.
Bur.		Place

WIFE'S FATHER JAMES HEALEY
WIFE'S MOTHER FLORENCE ROGERS
WIFE'S OTHER HUSBANDS JOHN FREDERIC HUGHES DIV. 22 AUG 1918
M. 20 MAY 1918

SEX M/F	CHILDREN Given Names SURNAME	WHEN BORN DAY MONTH YEAR	WHERE BORN TOWN	COUNTY	STATE OR COUNTRY	DATE OF FIRST MARRIAGE TO WHOM	WHEN DIED DAY MONTH YEAR
1	GEORGE ALFRED	30 OCT 1919					
2	ROSA MABEL	6 MAY 1922				GLEN MERL	
3	MELVA FRANCIS	16 JULY 1924				WILLIAM JOHN CHARSE	
4	JOHN RAYMOND HUGH	13 OCT 1928	NORTH MELB.	VIC	AUST	JOHN WILSON 14 JUNE 1952 / MYRA ELSA RICHARDSON 26 MAR 1962	
5	TERRANCE JAMES	3 OCT 1929				KATH	
6	RONALD MAXWELL	15 JUL 1934				KATH	
7	NOYCE ALWIN	7 MAY 1936				JEFFRY CALBY	
8	ROGER ARTHUR DRAKE	(FEB 1940 DIED)					
9	Margaret	(30/12 1928 DIED)					
10	(Betty) Shirley	(1937 DIED)					
11							

SOURCES OF INFORMATION

OTHER MARRIAGES

FAMILY GROUP RECORD

HUSBAND	WILLIAM DRAKE			Husband
Born	1837	Place	COUNTY DOWN IRELAND (TOWNLAND GLOUGH)	Wife
Chr.		Place		Ward
Marr.	8 AUG 1860	Place	ENGLWOOD COTTAGE, INVERLIEGH ALLANSFORD VICTORIA	Examiners
Died	1903	Place		Stake or Mission
Bur.		Place		

HUSBAND'S FATHER
HUSBAND'S MOTHER
HUSBAND'S OTHER WIVES

WIFE	ELIZABETH PERKINS		
Born	1844	Place	MELB. VICTORIA
Chr.		Place	
Died	1931	Place	CHELTENHAM, VIC
Bur.		Place	

WIFE'S FATHER   JOSEPH PERKINS
WIFE'S MOTHER   ELIZABETH ATT
WIFE'S OTHER HUSBANDS

SEX M/F	CHILDREN Given Names SURNAME	WHEN BORN DAY	MONTH	YEAR	WHERE BORN TOWN	COUNTY	STATE OR COUNTRY	DATE OF FIRST MARRIAGE TO WHOM	WHEN DIED DAY	MONTH	YEAR
1	MARYANN			1862	BARRABOOL VIC PAST					GEELONG	1992
2	JANE	12	JAN	1864	WILLIAM ROBERT GALLOWAY			1891		PARKVILLE VIC	1947
3	HUGH	12	DEC	1865	MARGARET EMILY BOLDON			1890		SOUTHMEAD	1916
4	ROBERT			1869	JANE MARION ELIZABETH MAHANY CHRISTIAN ROBERT MAHANY			15 JAN 1913			13 SEP 1925
5	ISABELLA MARGARET			1871	TEILING VIC			1872		BALLARAT	1961
6	JOSEPH	17	MAR	1874	ANNIE JANE LITTLE			1888		WARRAGOUL VIC	
7	MARGARET ELIZABETH			1879	ALFRED WILLIAM FOSTER			1902		BRIGHTON	1870
8											
9											
10											
11											

SOURCES OF INFORMATION

OTHER MARRIAGES

HUSBAND HUGH DRAKE

Born 12 DEC 1865 Place ALLANSFORD, VIC. AUST

Chr. Place

Marr. 15 OCT 1890 Place LINTON, VICTORIA.

Died Place

Bur. Place

Husband's Father DRAKE WILLIAM Husband's Mother ELIZABETH PERKINS

Husband's Other Wives

WIFE BOLDEN, HARRIET EMILY

Born 4 OCT 1867 Place WANGOON, VICTORIA, AUST

Chr. Place

Died Place

Bur. Place

Wife's Father BOLDEN WILLIAM Wife's Mother ELIZABETH HARRIS

Wife's Other Husbands

Husband	
Wife	
Ward	1
Examiners	2
Stake or Mission	

SEX M F	CHILDREN List each child (whether living or dead) in order of birth Given Names SURNAME	WHEN BORN			WHERE BORN			DATE OF FIRST MARRIAGE TO WHOM	WHEN DIED		
		DAY	MONTH	YEAR	TOWN	COUNTY	STATE OR COUNTRY		DAY	MONTH	YEAR
1	ETHEL										
2	HERBERT										
3	EPHRAIM										
4	ARTHUR	9	FEB	1900				3 JULY 1918 JOYCE ELLEN HEALEY	21	JULY	1969
5											
6											
7											
8											
9											
10											
11											

OTHER MARRIAGES

SOURCES OF INFORMATION

HUSBAND HUGH DRAKE

Born	1809	Place HILLSBOROUGH COUNTY DOWN IRELAND
Chr.	1836	Place
Mar.	14 APRIL 1890	Place ALLANSFORD VIC
Died		Place
Bur.		Place

HUSBAND'S FATHER WILLIAM BLAKE   HUSBAND'S MOTHER SARAH JOHNSON

HUSBAND'S OTHER WIVES

WIFE ANN JANE MARTIN

Born	1815	Place IRELAND
Chr.		Place
Died	5 AUG 1870	Place
Bur.		Place

WIFE'S FATHER WILLIAM MARTIN   WIFE'S MOTHER MARGARET

WIFE'S OTHER HUSBANDS

Husband
Wife
Ward
Examiners 1.
2
Stake or Mission

SEX M/F	CHILDREN List each child (whether living or dead) in order of birth Given Names / SURNAME	WHEN BORN			WHERE BORN			DATE OF FIRST MARRIAGE TO WHOM	STATE OR COUNTRY	WHEN DIED		
		DAY	MONTH	YEAR	TOWN	COUNTY				DAY	MONTH	YEAR
1	WILLIAM			1836	TOWNLAND CLOUGH	DOWN	IRELAND	8 AUG 1860 ELIZABETH PERKINS				
2	MARGARET			1838	"							
3	JOHN			1840	"			MARIA McDONALD		31 1 1914		
4	JAMES			1842	"							
5	HUGH			1847	"			AGNES RAYNEY (29 SEP 1894)		24 OCT 1923		
6	THOMAS			1849	"			FLORINA		9 JULY 1923		
7										(28 DEC 1950)		
8												
9												
10												
11												

OTHER MARRIAGES

SON of THOMAS — ALAN ARTHUR
DIED 4TH FEB 1925
AGED 11yrs

SOURCES OF INFORMATION

© 1972 The Genealogical Society of The Church of Jesus Christ of Latter-day Saints, Inc.
Deseret Book Company, Salt Lake City, Utah

Kerry .S. Drake

Personal Journal

Of

Sister Kerry Susan Drake
My memories of Childhood, Youth and Adulthood

From Fifteenth of January *19*87 (54). Y.B
to Twenty Sixth of December *19*78

My personal Journal will consist of the events and stages of my personal growth, which I think, need to be included within a personal history from my babyhood to childhood, Adolescent and also Adulthood etc.

My full name is Kerry Susan Drake.
I was born in the year Nineteen Hundred and Fifty Four on the Twenty fourth day of November. My sign therefore is Sagittarius

I record my first knowledge of life at an early age of 5,6,7 where in I dwelt in the homely suburbs of North Carlton, Melbourne – Victoria, Australia.

The address of that home is 23, Nicholous Street.
A small cottage which is early Victorian style.

My parents, that is Mum & Dad.
At that stage already were the
Parents of a little girl named 'Cheryl'
at my birth, and she is as you may already assume my elder sister.
Here is a picture of her in the hands of Dad.

2 Years

This is a picture of myself and my sister Cheryl at a very tender age
As you can see, we were visiting Father Christmas I'm the one on
My sister's right sitting on father
Christmas's knee I certainly was
cute then as you can see I
certainly wasn't amused at
my present yet I did enjoy
getting my picture taken.
My sister Cheryl Marie Drake
was Born 15.Aug.1953.
(She looks quiet & shy)

       Hugh Drake Joyce & George

HERE is a picture of my Mother and Father on their wedding day and a genealogical history of their heritage

John Raymond Hugh Drake
b. 13 Oct 1928
w. North Melbourne
m. 14 June 1952
d. 26 Mar 1962
w. Melb Mont park hospice

father Arther Joseph Drake
b. 8 Feb 1900
w. Warrigal
m. 3 July 1918
d. 21 July 1969

mother Joyce Ellen Healey
b. 29 March 1898
w.
d. 3 Jan 1955

Marie Elsa Richardson
b. 24 Apr 1933
w. Orbost Victoria
m. 14 June 1952
d. 25 Dec 1997
w. Alfred Hospital

father Henry Richardson
b. 22 June 1902
w. Newstead
m. 29 November 1924
d. 20 Feb 1973

mother Elsie Claudine Mustard
b. 14 November 1907
w. Bomballa NSW
d. 25 April 1965

5 years

As I relate to you the history of my life, it seems he memories of early childhood can only be captured through certain events which brings to life the relationships that I had developed as a child.

That is I knew not my mom & dad in personality, I'm sure these influences has rubbed off on me and also their example because to this day I can appreciate all they have given me in this life. My father John Raymond Hugh Drake was a well loved man before I was born, possessed with many good qualities and talents as a person he was admired by all his family & friends. As a man I imagine he was fairly intelligent and also carried himself with respect for his achievements in life, a great sportsman and also personally earned him many awards for "Best &" in his sports.

Unfortunately at an early age of 33 my father was involved in a bad car crash, it seems that unfortunate as it may seem God knew he was needed for another purpose on the other side. He was thrown out of the car and hit his head on the concrete pavement.

Brain damage left him a vegetable and he died later in the Mount Park Hospital. I can recall visiting my father as we were only young. My father used to refer to us as his three little girls at that stage- Myshelle had come along and by this time, she would have been 3-4 yrs old. B. 9.12.58.
I could see my father's face and the only thing that struck me was my father was sick and dying. He was so white, the bed was made of iron and the walls were pale too - it was eerie. I could see that he did not fully know us. A tragic time for my mother and family.

The only important even that occurred
in my life with Dad, was one day
when he was leaving for work
was he kissed the cat goodbye
on the table- after he kissed
me and said he'd bring me
a bike home for my Birthday.

~6 Years~

I remember laughing because this
seemed to me to be my dad's
personality and I had a great love
for his good character & his eagerness
to please me at that age.

Another event that I can recall is the time I received a cigarette burn on
my neck, I remember or I have been told that whilst sitting on a friend
of a family's knee, he was cuddling me, he mistakened my neck for his
mouth, it seems to mehe must have been half waked – at the time.

Another event in my early childhood was the time that
I nearly left this life - Oh you see it was one of those days when I was
visiting my auntie's and she left me alone for some time. Apparently
while showering with her husband I got my dummy stuck down my
throat and began to turn a shade of blue & black. My aunty maintains,
has never forgotten the day, and as you may have guessed, I am still
alive, a close shave with Death as a 'Babe'

I do remember greatly my grandfather and mother especially grandma,
we used to visit her quiet often and fight over who was going to stay
for the weekend.
My grandma was a great cook, beautiful scones, and cakes and also
she was the best grandmother in the world to me. I recall one morning
when grandpa had left for work and grandma told me to climb in bed
with her she began to tell some stories about the time she used to shoot
rabbits and when she used to ride a white horse down the street which

had no saddle and reins. She said all she had to do was turn the horse's head in the direction she wanted to go and he would go.

We spent some great time together. I can recall that my Aunty Jean and cousins Lee & Michael lived in the next commission flat in Heidelberg Lee & Michael used to fight like cats & dogs,

Aunty Jean was a good persone. She used to give us clothes. - I can remember Lee & Michael had no dad either and although they were in this situation they lived better than we did.

Lee went to a catholic school Saint Pius, I was sent to a state school and I remember when my dad died, I was moved around quite a bit from Aunty to Grandma for some reason.

There was some problems in the family. At this time I came into contact with my Aunty Barbara and Roy, whom I loved dearly, they were great. Also Judy & Peter & Graham, who were their children. I understand that my Aunty Barbara loved me a great deal and that she wanted to adopt me. But I used to say NO! I want to go home to mummy and daddy. They lived in Burwood 9 Moona st. A lovely house, modern. Aunty Barbara was also a good cook, I enjoyed having her make my favorite biscuits ANZACS- They were especially made for me everytime I visited Aunty Barbara. They also had a little puppy dog named BO.BO. He was ugly & pug nosed like a bull dog but he was a good dog.

Judy was good to me as I used to sleep in her room. I remember my first stay with them, my aunty bought me a tartan skirt and cardigan plus lots of games to play with while I was staying in with them.

Graham & Peter were much older and they were great too.

I remember Peter used to pick on me, but Graham and I got on terrific, he was like a big brother to me. I used to sit on the couch and comb his hair.

But those days son ended, as my mother remarried or found another man- his name was frank and he came from Ireland. And he was also bald.

A big strong looking person- I didn't like him at all, I guess I was a bit jealous- not unusual for a child of my age too.

Well anyway I recall our first encounter with our new father was when we all moved to Box Hill. to live, we lived in the gigantic house – it was I learnt at that time a Private Hospital, we were renting the front part which was huge – there was only 2 bedrooms, one which mum & Frank used and the other us three little girls in a little tiny room with only one bed, oh did we complain as we had to sleep together and it was very annoying – I can recall meal times were very sober as we had to eat everything and go to bed.

I can also recall us playing table tennis on one of the big tables in the lounge- and also the fact that there was an orange tree outside which I think we used to pinch the oranges.

I can recall also attending a primary school in Box hill.

I used to recall ordering my lunch and somehow we used to have to use those funny coins with a hole in the center.

It was also at this school that I can recall I had my learning tested and about this time that it was noticed that I needed glasses. I used to knock into things occasionally you see.

Then we moved from B.H. We were there only for a short time.
There was a problem you see, I think the rent was too high or we were told to leave because the lady found out there were more than 3 children. Mum was having a baby and we moved to Patterson at Carlton. And I started to attend Princess Hill Primary school.

I was in grade 2 now and soon my mother had a baby girl. Us children grew quick. Kathy was a beautiful little girl. B.
I can recall us looking after her a lot of times.
And even when mom didn't come home for days we had to do most of the grown up jobs.
Frank with his Irish rage and alcohol, do not make a happy home for children.

I was teacher's pet in Grade three- and used to walk with her around the school ground picking up rubbish.

I liked her a lot, I can't recall her name it could have been Miss Robin or something like that.

She left at the end of that year as she was having a baby.
Grade 4 was an interesting year apparently our class was the mischief class-and so we were informed that we were sent to Mr. Ludlow for repentance.

What a teacher Mr. Ludlow was, he was in his early 50s, tall thing, he walked like a soldier headmaster and a very distinctive bounce or lift which I can still imitate these days.

Another remarkable feature about this man was his unusual temper, boy, when he would get mad his face would go red and his bone or vein would stick out in the middle of his forehead.

One of his good moments and unusual talents was during our cooking classes, we used to make things and eat them afterwards.
One day we were to make bread, unfortunately we made it on a fry pan, and you know what happened don't you? It turned out a hard as a rock.

I learnt a lot in 4th grade especially about maths. We did so many times tables, I knew them off by heart.
I remember once when a young boy named Bruno B. did something bad in class and instead of strapping him- he turned the boy upside down and held him in the air until all the blood ran to his face.
It wasn't punishment, it was torture.
I'll never forget Mr. Ludlow

Grade 5 was wonderful at Princess st state school.

Why I guess I was starting to do well in class, we had a good teacher Mr. Mullet; he would often hold competitions and the winners would receive a snowball or a something nice. He was friendly and a good example.

We didn't stay very long in Patterson street, we moved from the corner flat we lived in to a little terrace house two streets down. We were poor in the things of the world, also I can recall Kathy growing and some of the friends we used to have in the streets – the parties we would have, the trips to the football and the park, the concerts and all that we used to enjoy in the spare time.

Well time moved on and again we moved. I must tell you, this was a big problem changing schools and doing many things that disrupted life continually. Although what could I do about it. My mother was having a rough time with Frank or they were both giving each other a rough time. Well then my Grandmother died and oh I was so sad. 25 April ANZAC day. My mother of course was sad about it too. I remember crying because she was so good. She used to look after us many times during the time when Mum & dad were fighting and mum would decide to leave home & take us. It was a shock for all my Aunties Fay, Jean, and Susie, the youngest who I used to play with. Well grandmother was a dearly missed person. One thing I can recall and that is mum would tell us often of how she had to pay for the funeral.

Apparently after my dad's accident- death, 3ʳᵈ party _____ had come through and mum had some money that could be spent.

Have you ever known anyone that has had more sorrow than happiness- well I guess my mother faced some trials – not only did I feel for her but I cried a lot about all the things that used to happen to her. When it's your mother, you want to protect them.

I guess it was about now or even earlier than this that I started to grow 'mutinations' In many ways I started to think a lot and ask why?

We were christened cahotlics- also church was not on or calendar or prayers who was God I'd ask-
We did move to Thornbury my mother put money on a house there and we moved in- Frank was with us and we not attended Fairfeild North Primary school.
A new school and a new teacher in 5th grade.
Miss TOBIN was horrible and crabby and intolerable to you if you made mistakes. I remember receiving my first strap as a girl from her. I was so hurt and afraid, I never made another mistake.
The work wasn't so hard, it was just, having to catch up as I had changed schools and we didn't stat till 2 wks after we had left the other school. I forgot what I had learnt and somehow what we were learning was harder. I wasn't a brain I was average couldn't really do much except draw which I was good at and assignments.
Life wasn't meant to be easy I learnt well. Time moved on and I got better, made few friends like Pat and Lillian and many others whom I can't all recall now.

"I recall my first impressions of God. When we had catechism Classes at Princess Primary School. I can recall asking the priest who visited and taught us. How did we get trees. How did God create trees?"

CPSIA information can be obtained
at www.ICGtesting.com
Printed in the USA
BVHW030928260719
554446BV00004B/30/P